AMAZING EARTH
Earthquakes

by Sandra Markle

Illustrations by Jo-Ellen C. Bosson

SCHOLASTIC INC.

New York   Toronto   London   Auckland   Sydney
Mexico City   New Delhi   Hong Kong   Buenos Aires

With admiration, for Don and Ruth Ferguson

CAN YOU BELIEVE...

NOTE TO PARENTS AND TEACHERS: This book is intended to help children develop skills and concepts related to the following processes: that earthquakes are part of how the earth's crust changes—both slowly and suddenly—when the plates forming the crust shift. Children will also see how technology is being used to monitor plate movement in the hope of warning people when a strong earthquake is likely. "The surface of the earth changes. Some changes are due to slow processes, such as erosion and weathering, and some changes are due to rapid processes, such as landslides, volcanic eruptions, and earthquakes." (National Science Education Standards as identified by the National Academy of Sciences for K-4 students.)

Can you believe

this house was destroyed by a process that started inside the earth?

This house in Rapar, India, crumpled during an earthquake on February 1, 2001. The little girl stayed safe by climbing inside a big metal pot. But what made the earth shake? And why did the ground tremble at just that spot instead of somewhere else on earth? This book will let you find out. You'll also explore why some earthquakes cause huge sea waves that smash into land. Along the way, you'll discover lots of amazing facts about earthquakes—some may even seem unbelievable!

Earth's surface is always changing. Sometimes those changes happen very slowly, like when a river carves its channel. Other times, like during an earthquake, those changes happen quickly.

So what made part of the earth's surface shake?

A. heat
B. wind
C. waves

Turn the page and start exploring to find out!

Can you believe

that heat deep inside the earth made the surface shake?

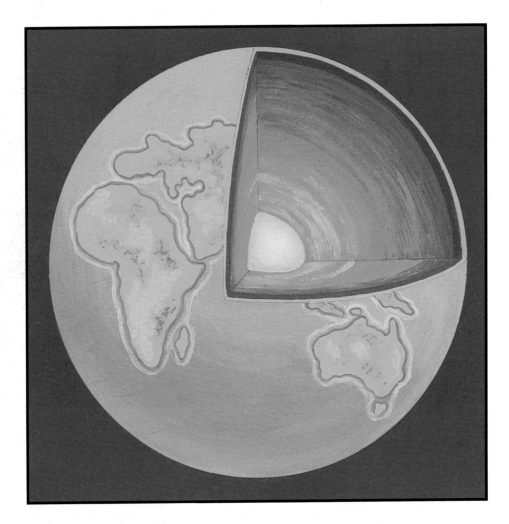

If you put a chocolate candy bar into a pan and heated it, what do you think would happen? As the candy warms up, the solid chocolate becomes a thick, soft paste. The **core** of the earth is much hotter than a stove—hot enough to melt rock. Because of this intense heat, much of the earth's interior, an area called the **mantle**, is made of a plasticlike rock material.

DID YOU KNOW?

Alaska has more than 5,000 earthquakes a year. That's more than the combined total for all of the other states in the United States.

Compared to the rest of its mass, the earth's crust is as thin as an eggshell. Like a dropped egg, the earth's crust is cracked into pieces called **plates**. But those plates aren't still.

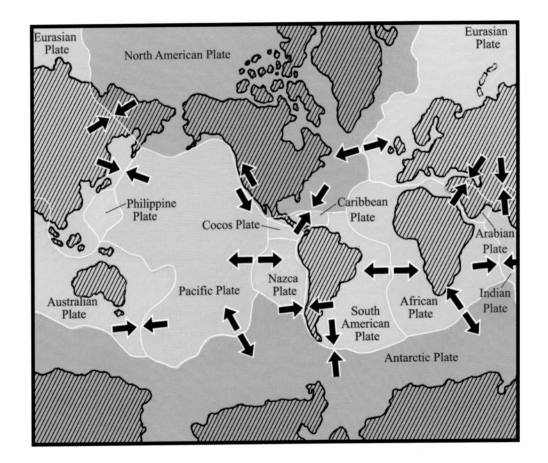

This map shows earth's plates, and the arrows show the direction each plate is moving. So what makes such huge pieces of the earth's crust move?

TRY IT YOURSELF!

Note: Be sure to ask permission to do the activities and have an adult help you with any activity using the stove.

1. To model what's happening under the plates, boil water in a saucepan on the stove.

2. Drop in four raisins.

You'll see the raisins sink, rise, and sink again. The raisins are riding the currents created by the water, which rises as it heats up and sinks as it cools.

The earth's hot core creates the same sort of currents in the mantle, although these flow extremely slowly. Scientists believe that the mantle's currents are also dragging along the earth's plates.

So what happens when two of these huge plates run into each other?

A. One plate crumples.
B. One plate sinks under the other.
C. One plate slides sideways.

Can you believe

the plates do all three?

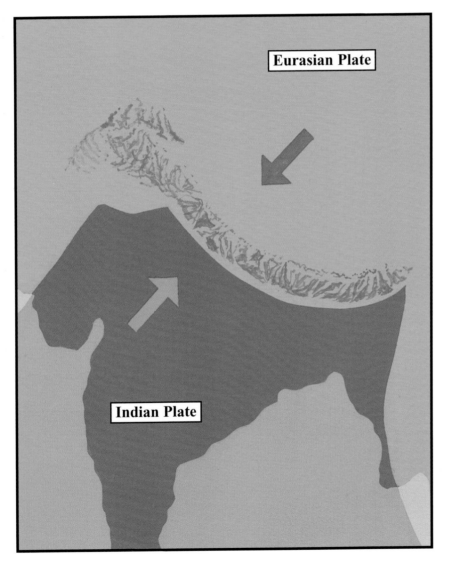

Eurasian Plate

Indian Plate

Sometimes when two plates run into each other, one plate crumples up into a mountain range. This map shows the mountain range that has formed where the Eurasian Plate and the Indian Plate push against each other.

DID YOU KNOW?

The tallest mountain on earth, Mount Everest, is 29,035 feet (8850 meters) and growing taller by about 2 inches (6 centimeters) a year. Think how much taller Mount Everest will be in a thousand years!

TRY IT YOURSELF!

Try this activity to see how two plates running into each other can create mountains.

1. Squeeze modeling clay between your hands to soften it.

2. Place the ball of clay on a piece of newspaper, and use a water-filled soft-drink bottle or a rolling pin to roll it flat.

3. Use a rock or a partner to anchor one end of the clay sheet.

4. Push, sliding the other end of the clay toward this anchor. You'll see the clay crumple.

That's the same way the earth's crust crumples, creating mountains.

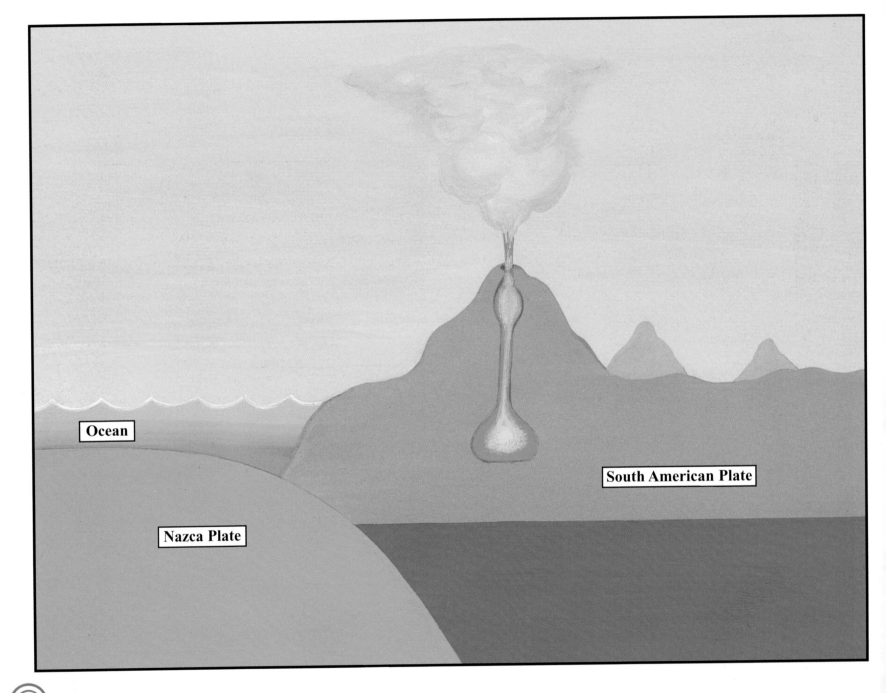

Ocean

South American Plate

Nazca Plate

If you could drain the Pacific Ocean and then fly over this area, you would see what else happens when two plates meet: One can slide under the other. When the plate forming the seafloor slides under the land-mass plate, deep trenches form.

This process created the Peru-Chile trench off the coast of South America. And as the Nazca Plate pushed under the South American Plate, land along the coast was uplifted. This created the Andes Mountains.

DID YOU KNOW?

One part of the **Mariana Trench**, near the Philippines, called the Challenger Deep, is deeper than Mount Everest is tall.

Volcanoes also often erupt where plates that form the seafloor sink under continental plates. Scientists think the friction of one plate rubbing against another generates enough heat to melt rock. This melted rock, called **magma**, rises through cracks or pushes rocks apart to reach the surface. Once at the surface, the molten magma is called **lava**. When the lava hardens and builds up layer upon layer, the result is a volcanic mountain.

DID YOU KNOW?

Volcanic islands, such as the Hawaiian Islands, are really just the tops of very tall mountains, stretching from the seafloor to the surface.

This lake, called Sag Pond, formed when land along the San Andreas Fault near Parkfield, California, shifted. The San Andreas Fault is a crack in the earth's crust where the North American Plate and the Pacific Plate bump together.

Since movement of the earth's plates is a natural process, when does this movement cause an earthquake?

A. when it happens suddenly

B. when it stops

C. when it goes in reverse

Can you believe

an earthquake happens when a plate shifts suddenly?

Even when one plate slides very slowly under the other, the two pieces of crust are likely to lock together from time to time. Then the pressure builds, like a rubber band being stretched until it finally breaks. When the locked plates break loose, part of the crust suddenly moves.

A portion of the southern coast of California is located on the Pacific Plate. The rest of California is on the North American Plate. To understand how these two plates are moving, put the palms of your hands together. Press your hands tightly against each other as you try to slide your right hand toward you. At first, your hand won't move. Then it's likely to move with a quick jerk.

DID YOU KNOW?

Scientists estimate land is moving along the San Andreas Fault in California at a rate of about 2 inches (56 millimeters) each year. That's about the same rate your fingernails grow.

Here you can see what happened on September 23, 1999, when an earthquake rocked Taipei, Taiwan. When the plate Taipei rests on moved, a tremble passed through soil and rock. The actual spot where the rocks break or shift may be deep underground or it may be close to the surface. The trembling is most severe at the **epicenter**, the spot on the surface directly above the action. Drop a pebble into a pan of water to see how the shock waves travel out from this spot in all directions, getting weaker as they go.

DID YOU KNOW?

People felt the 1994 Bolivian earthquake as far away as Renton, Washington. That's about 5,400 miles (8700 kilometers)—a record for sensing earthquake tremors.

Look at the damage caused
by the March 27, 1964,
Alaskan earthquake.
When the earth shifted, it
released as much energy as
240 million tons of TNT.

In some places, the ground was
lifted up as much as 56 feet
(17 meters)!

Here you can see the damage a weaker earthquake caused in Los Angeles, California, in 1994. How much weaker was this quake than the 1964 Alaskan quake? To help people evaluate and compare, Charles Richter developed a scale for ranking earthquakes. Every higher number on the Richter scale represents a release of about thirty times more energy than the next lower number. Quakes measuring 2.0 or less usually aren't even felt. Quakes measuring up to 6.0 may cause minor damage. The 1964 Alaskan quake, which caused major damage, measured 9.2. The 1994 California quake measured 6.7.

DID YOU KNOW?

The strongest earthquake recorded to date was the 1960 Chilean quake. It had an estimated magnitude of 9.5.

What happens to buildings in an earthquake depends partly on what the ground is like underneath them. Sandy, loose soil magnifies the earthquake's wavelike motion, making buildings shake more. How well buildings hold together depends on how they were constructed.

Tall buildings on stilts, such as office towers with open, ground-floor parking, quickly weaken and topple. Buildings with overhanging floors are also likely to twist, breaking apart. When these buildings fall, they cause more damage, smashing into nearby stronger buildings. Earthquake damage is often worst in poorer countries. Buildings there are less likely to have steel bars reinforcing cement walls or to have the floors tied together at the corners, strengthening the whole structure.

Besides shaking the ground, earthquakes cause damage in another way. What is it?

A. Earthquakes produce strong winds.
B. Earthquakes cause heavy rains.
C. Earthquakes generate giant waves.

Can you believe

earthquakes can make giant waves?

If you've ever scooted back and forth in a bathtub, you've discovered how a sudden shift in the seafloor produces giant waves. Called **tsunami**, these huge ocean waves are generated when there is an undersea landslide. A landslide can be triggered by an earthquake or if the seafloor crust suddenly moves upward.

A 1993 tsunami that struck Okushhiri, Japan, was as high as an eight-story building. Tsunamis are also likely to roll ashore as a series of three or four giant waves as much as an hour apart. These waves crash down on buildings, bridges, harbors, and roads with tremendous force. Each wave sucks debris, land, and even people away as the water withdraws into the ocean again.

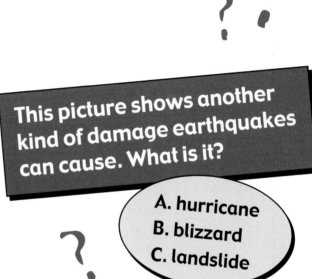

This picture shows another kind of damage earthquakes can cause. What is it?

A. hurricane
B. blizzard
C. landslide

Can you believe

earthquakes can cause land to slide downhill?

On January 13, 2001, a strong earthquake struck El Salvador. Not only did the earthquake damage buildings, it set off 249 landslides. This one in Santa Tecla, near San Salvador, was one of the worst. The earthquake made the hillside slump and the soil flow like a river. Uprooted trees and rocks acted like battering rams, smashing into buildings, bridges, and cars. Meanwhile, the mud buried everything in its path.

Sometimes, earthquakes can trigger fires by breaking gas lines. That can cause even more damage than the shifting earth. This fire started in Los Angeles after the January 17, 1994, earthquake. A spark was enough to ignite gas leaking from burst pipes. Because the earthquake had broken water pipes, firefighting crews were unable to get enough water pressure to put out the fire.

One of the world's most famous earthquakes, the 1906 San Francisco quake, also started one of the most destructive fires. Survivors said the earth seemed to buck and jump during the quake. Dishes, furniture, and people were tossed about, windows crashed to the pavement, and whole buildings collapsed. As people fled into the street, afraid more quakes would follow, a fire started, probably from a toppled stove. The wind quickly spread the flames. The quake probably lasted less than a minute, but the fire raged for three days. By the time the fire was out, many buildings that survived the quake were also rubble.

DID YOU KNOW?

Earthquake waves move through the earth at 3 miles (about 5 kilometers) per second. That's too fast to outrun!

This woman was one of the lucky ones after an earthquake caused heavy damage in Pereira, Colombia, on January 25, 1999. Rescuers heard her cries for help and freed her from the rubble.

As soon as a quake is over, people have to pull together to rescue those who are trapped. The first people on the scene can only pull away the rubble with their hands. The earthquake will probably have cut off electricity and buried heavy equipment, such as bulldozers. It's important to find and free injured people as quickly as possible. Within hours, help is usually on its way from neighboring cities—even from other countries. Special rescue teams even bring dogs that are trained to sniff out people buried beneath fallen debris. Next, government agencies and international relief organizations, like the Red Cross, bring tents, food, water, and clothes to help the survivors start to recover. Because there are thousands of earthquakes every year and as many as fifteen cause significant damage, it's no wonder people want to find a way to predict quakes.

? ? ? ? ?

How do researchers try to do that?

A. watching animals
B. using seismographs
C. using lasers

Can you believe

researchers use all three methods to predict earthquakes?

Researchers at the United States Geological Survey (USGS) don't believe in animal behavior as a quake predictor, but some people do. According to folklore, unproven ideas people have and pass down from generation to generation, the number of dogs howling and running away from home goes up before an earthquake. Some people also believe other animals, such as snakes, bees, and catfish, detect earthquake waves. However, no scientific studies have been able to prove that snakes crawl out of underground dens, bees leave their hives, or catfish leap out of lakes more often than usual before an earthquake.

Watching animal behavior has saved lives. On February 4, 1975, the Chinese evacuated the city of Haicheng mainly because researchers thought they saw animals behaving strangely. A few hours later, a strong quake struck Haicheng, destroying nearly ninety percent of the buildings. However, this may have been just a coincidence.

Since then, scientists have not been able to use animal behavior to predict major earthquakes. Researchers are having more luck studying what small earthquakes may tell us about what's going on within the earth's crust. This information could be used to forecast large earthquakes.

One of the earliest instruments researchers invented to study movements of the earth's crust is the seismometer. Early models had a heavy weight on a spring attached to a frame that was anchored to the ground. This instrument was attached to a seismograph, a recording device as simple as a pen, marking a revolving roll of paper. Anytime the ground moved, the seismometer moved and the ink line spiked—the stronger the quake, the bigger the spike. Today, seismometers can detect even the tiniest earth motions, called microquakes. A computer records the motion.

TRY IT YOURSELF!

Follow these steps to build a model seismometer and see how it works.

1. Tie a 2-foot (about 60-centimeter) piece of string to one end of a ruler. Tie the free end of the string to the middle of a marking pen. Tape this end to the pen so it stays in place.

2. Press a ball of modeling clay as big around as a Ping-Pong ball over the taped string. Use books to anchor the ruler so the string hangs over the side of a table.

3. Place a roll of paper towels so the marker's tip touches the paper.

Have a partner jiggle the table while you slowly slide the paper towels past the marker.

One problem researchers face is shake pollution, movement caused by machines like rumbling subway trains and blasting to build roads.

Researchers have learned to pay attention when movement along a fault stops. That can mean the plates have locked up and the pressure is likely to build up until the locked section breaks free. The result could be a major earthquake. So now researchers are using lasers and a satellite to watch faults. Called LAGEOS II, the satellite is covered with 426 reflectors. About thirty countries share this satellite, bouncing laser beams off its surface. By measuring how long it takes a beam to return to its source, researchers can determine the exact location of that point. Because LAGEOS II is constantly orbiting earth, researchers around the world can check the position of points along faults many times each month.

Researchers can also analyze signals given off by the GPS (Global Positioning System) network to measure exact points on the earth's surface. These satellites are usually used to help people find their destination. But they can also be used to monitor faults. This information could possibly be used to warn people that a strong earthquake is likely.

But is there anything people can do to be prepared for an earthquake?

A. They can get in shape to outrun the quake.

B. They can build earthquake-resistant buildings.

C. They can build machines to stop the earth from moving.

Can you believe

people are constructing buildings that can survive earthquakes?

In the past, some researchers have tried to reduce the chance of earthquakes by pumping water and mud into faults. The idea was to keep the crust's plates from locking up. But this effort didn't seem to help. Researchers have also considered forcing the crust apart at faults with high-pressure steam. But no one is sure this would work, either. So other researchers have focused on designing buildings that can ride out a quake.

DID YOU KNOW?

Florida and North Dakota have recorded the fewest earthquakes in the United States. Alaska has recorded the most. That's because Alaska is on the boundary between two plates. Florida and North Dakota are in the middle of the North American Plate.

One way to protect a building from earthquakes is to give the building a broad supporting base and a pyramid shape to make it more flexible. The Trans American Building in San Francisco, seen in the picture above, uses this technique. The 44-story Torre Latinoamericana Building in Mexico proved that another approach also works. Built of concrete reinforced with steel bars, the Torre building remained sound while surrounding buildings crumpled during the 1985 Mexico City quake. Since then, other tall buildings in earthquake-prone areas have been built with steel-reinforced concrete walls.

Another way to help a building ride out an earthquake is to give it a movable base. The building sits on layers of steel and an elastic material. This way, the building easily slides from side to side, riding the earthquake waves. The first building to have a movable base, the Law & Justice Center in San Bernardino, California, has successfully survived several minor earthquakes undamaged. Other buildings with movable bases have now been built in earthquake-prone areas such as Japan, Indonesia, New Zealand, and Armenia.

Can you believe

you can prepare for an earthquake?

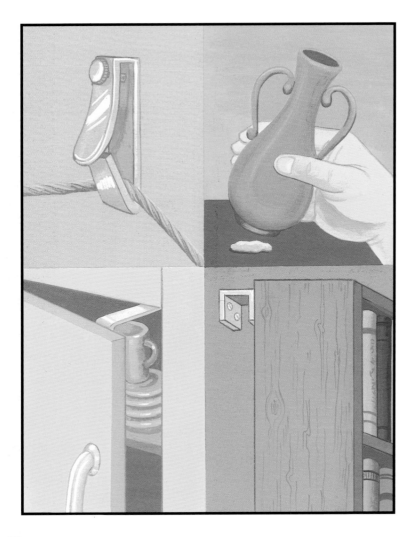

Since earthquakes can happen anywhere, it's good to be prepared no matter where you live. You and your parents can go on a hazard hunt around your house. Look for things that could hurt if they fell on you and things that would break if knocked to the floor. Make sure pictures and mirrors stay on walls by hanging them on closed wall hooks instead of nails. Glass and pottery objects can be anchored with special putty that you can buy at hardware stores. Because dishes and pots and pans can fall off shelves, make sure cupboard doors have latches. If they don't, your family can add latches. Bookcases and tall cupboards also need to be attached to walls.

DID YOU KNOW?

You'd even need to prepare for earthquakes on the moon. But studies show moonquakes happen less often and are weaker than quakes on earth.

You and your parents can put together an earthquake kit, supplies your family may need after an earthquake. This kit should include:

- bottled water—one gallon (about 5 liters) per person per day for a week
- a first aid kit
- canned food that can be eaten without cooking
- can opener (nonelectric)
- blankets or sleeping bags
- battery-operated radio and spare batteries
- flashlight and spare batteries
- any prescription drugs your family needs
- extra eyeglasses for anyone who wears glasses
- fire extinguisher
- if there is a baby in your family, be sure to include baby food, clothes, and disposable diapers

If there is an earthquake, don't panic. Duck under a table or other shelter, stand in a doorway, or crouch down and cover your head. Remember, most quakes last less than a minute. Stay under cover for a few minutes after the shaking stops, in case of aftershocks, additional quakes that may follow the first one. Be sure your family has a plan for where to meet or how to get together again after an earthquake. Then you'll be prepared and know what to do in case of an earthquake.

In this picture, Jeffrey Freymueller is checking a GPS (Global Positioning System) unit. He said, "Once I have the GPS units in place, I can use these to measure the exact location of points on the earth's surface. Over time, I can measure exactly how much those points shift." Jeffrey Freymueller is an earth detective, trying to solve a big mystery—how much and how often the earth's plates shift along faults.

This GPS unit is at the base of Mount Everest, earth's tallest mountain. Jeffrey Freymueller said, "I'm studying the collision of the earth's plates in this area and how the crust responds to that collision. I've even been able to check the movement of points on Mount Everest as high as the last camp before people climb to the summit." One thing Freymueller has learned is that the motion of the crust in the area known as India is causing slipping along faults. Because of that, the Himalayan Mountains are continuing to be uplifted. He said, "I'd like to learn how to use movement along faults as clues to predict major earthquakes everywhere in the world."

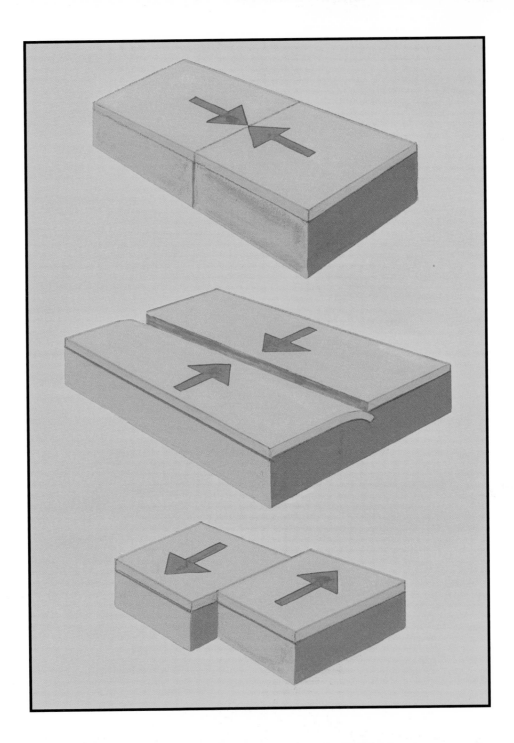

Can you believe

earthquakes are part of earth's natural processes?

The processes that make the earth's crust move are part of what happens when the earth's hot core melts rock material in the mantle, making it flow. This naturally makes pieces of the crust move, bumping into each other, slipping under or over each other, or sliding alongside each other. In an earthquake, this movement happens suddenly and violently. It makes buildings collapse and makes huge, damaging waves. So while earthquakes are the result of earth's natural processes, these super shakes are those processes gone wild!

Glossary/Index/Pronunciation Guide

core [KOOR] The center of the earth. 4, 7

epicenter [EP-pih-SEN-tehr] The area of the earth's surface directly above the site where rocks broke, causing an earthquake. 17

fault [FAWLT] A crack in the rocks that form the earth's crust, along which one side has moved relative to the other in response to stress. 14, 34, 36, 43

fire [FYE-uhr] The light, heat, and flames produced by something burning. 25-27

Global Positioning System (GPS) [GLOW-buhl puh-ZISH-uhn-ing SIS-tuhm] Units used to receive a signal from orbiting satellites in order to determine the precise location of a set of points on the earth's surface. 35, 43

lava [LA-vuh] Melted rock that flows out of an active volcano. 13

landslide [LAND-SLIDE] Soil, rocks, or mud moving downhill. 23-24

magma [MAG-muh] Molten rock material within the earth. 13

mantle [MAN-tuhl] The part of the earth that lies between the crust and the core. 4, 7

Mariana Trench [MAR-ee-AH-nuh TRENCH] Located southwest of Guam in the western Pacific Ocean, this is the ocean's deepest trench. 11

Mount Everest [MOWNT EV-uh-rist] At 29,035 feet (8850 meters) this mountain in the Himalayas is the tallest mountain on earth. 8

plate [PLAYT] Part of the earth's crust that can move separately. 5-11, 13-15, 22, 36, 42-44

prediction [pruh-DIK-shun] A statement about something that is likely to happen in the future, such as a warning that a major earthquake is likely to occur. 30-35, 42-44

preparedness [prih-PAYR-uhd-ness] The process of being ready for action, such as preparing for a major earthquake. 37-41

rescue [RES-kyoo] To save someone from a dangerous or harmful situation, such as a major earthquake. 28-29

Richter Scale [RIK-tur SKAYL] A scale developed by Charles Richter to measure the amount of energy released by earthquakes. 19-20

San Andreas Fault [SAN an-DRAY-uhs FAWLT] A fault zone stretching from San Francisco, south to San Diego, where the North American Plate and the Pacific Plate slide along each other. 14-15

satellite [SAT-uh-lite] Object put into orbit around the earth for relaying communication signals or to collect and transmit data. 34-35

seismograph [SIZE-muh-graf] A recording device attached to a seismometer to record when the earth's crust moves. 32-33

seismometer [size-MOM-muh-tur] Instrument to detect when the earth's crust moves. 32

trench [TRENCH] Deep, steep-sided valley in the seafloor. 10-11

tsunami [tsoo-NAH-mee] A big, destructive ocean wave caused by a shift in the seafloor crust. 21-22

volcano [vol-KAY-no] A mountain created by the buildup of volcanic material. 12-13

PHOTO CREDITS:

Cover: (top left) Robert Yager/Stone/Getty Images;
(middle left) Michael Dwyer/Associated Press;
(bottom left) La Prensa Gráfica/Associated Press;
(right) Anat Givon/Associated Press

p. 3: Sherwin Crasto/Associated Press

p. 5: Skip Jeffery

p. 12: Tui De Roy

p. 14: Michael Andrews/Animals Animals/Earth Scenes

p. 16: Anat Givon/Associated Press

p. 18 (both): Consortium Library,
University of Alaska, Anchorage

p. 19: Eric Draper/Associated Press

p. 21: Michael Dwyer/Associated Press

p. 23: La Prensa Gráfica/Associated Press

p. 25: Lenny Ignelzi/Associated Press

p. 26 (both): Associated Press

p. 28: Oswaldo Paez/Associated Press

p. 32: Skip Jeffery

p. 35: NOAA

p. 37: Lee Foster/Bruce Coleman Inc.

p. 42: Qizhi Chen, University of Alaska

p. 43: Freysteinn Sigmundsson, Nordic Volcanologic Institute,
Reykjavik, Iceland

Acknowledgments: The author would like to thank the following persons for sharing their expertise and enthusiasm: Dr. Neville Hudson, Geology Department, University of Auckland, New Zealand; Dr. Kent Lindquist and Dr. Jeffrey T. Freymueller, Geophysical Institute, University of Alaska. As always, a special thanks to Skip Jeffery for his help and support.

ISBN 0-439-35614-8

Text copyright © 2002 by Sandra Markle.
Illustrations copyright © 2002 by Scholastic Inc.

All rights reserved.
Published by Scholastic Inc., 557 Broadway, New York, NY 10012.
SCHOLASTIC and associated logos are trademarks
and/or registered trademarks of Scholastic Inc.

12 11 10 9 8 7 6 5 4 3 2 1   2 3 4 5 6 7/0

Printed in the U.S.A.
First printing, October 2002